The AWESOMEST, MOST AMAZING, MOST EPIC MOVIE GUIDE

in the universe!

LEGO

THE LEGO MOVIE 2

The AWESOMEST, MOST AMAZING, MOST EPIC MOVIE GUIDE

in the universe!

Written by
Helen Murray

CONTENTS

INTRODUCTION

Aliens from the DUPLO planet attack Bricksburg. They smash buildings, crush everything in their path, and blast off into space with bricks. Emmet and his brave group of friends work together to rebuild the city and to defend their home. But the brick-looting aliens keep coming back for more! Can the heroes stop them?

"We are from the **DUPLO** planet and we are here to destroy you!"

—DUPLO planet aliens

APOCALYPSEBURG

Bricksburg is now a dusty, brick-strewn city known as Apocalypseburg. No matter how many times the citizens rebuild their beloved home, the DUPLO aliens return to destroy it.

STOLEN BRICKS

The aliens gobble up bricks and beam them into space. The citizens do not know what they are up to—but the aliens are taking the bricks to Queen Watevra Wa'Nabi, the ruler of the Systar System in outer space.

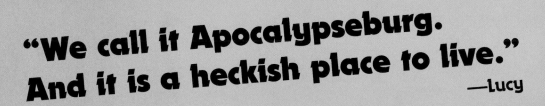

"We call it Apocalypseburg. And it is a heckish place to live."
—Lucy

QUICK, RUN!

Terrified citizens and their pets flee. They eventually lose hope that anything can ever return to how it was.

NEW THREAT

Now, a strange, new alien ship has arrived in Apocalypseburg. Its mysterious pilot, Sweet Mayhem, takes Emmet's friends! She flies them to the Systar System to meet the Queen. What does she want with them?

A GUIDE TO SURVIVING LIFE IN APOCALYPSEBURG

Apocalypseburg is a heckish place to live. Its citizens no longer follow rules, and there is always a risk of alien attack. Only the toughest can survive!

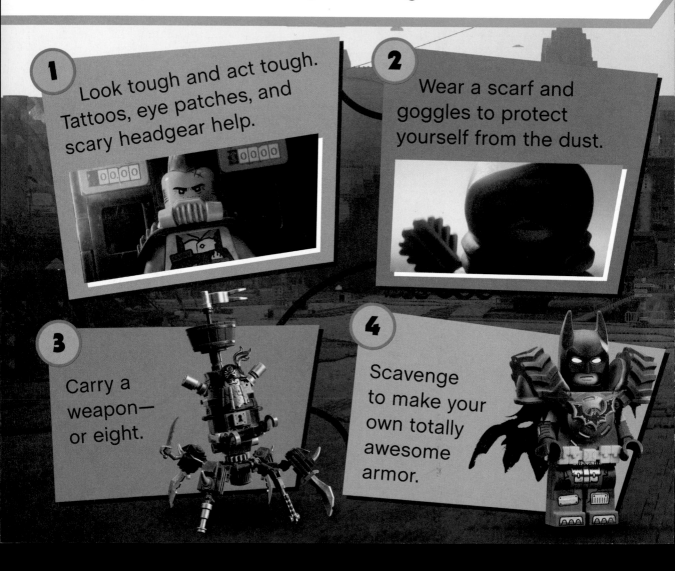

1 Look tough and act tough. Tattoos, eye patches, and scary headgear help.

2 Wear a scarf and goggles to protect yourself from the dust.

3 Carry a weapon— or eight.

4 Scavenge to make your own totally awesome armor.

5 Always keep an eye out for any new alien attacks.

6 Stick together with your friends at all times.

7 Drink overpriced coffee when it all gets to be too much.

13

"This new life has toughened and hardened us all. Well ... toughened most of us."

—Lucy

EMMET

Life in Apocalypseburg may be tough, but Emmet Brickowski always manages to stay cheerful. He works hard to rebuild his town—he just wants to make everything awesome again.

THINGS YOU NEED TO KNOW ABOUT EMMET

1 Emmet is a Master Builder. He uses the bricks around him to build whatever he needs.

2 Emmet saved the universe a few years ago by taking on the then-evil Lord Business and the destructive "man upstairs."

3 Friends are very important to Emmet. His best friend is Lucy.

4 He takes his coffee with a touch of cream—and 25 sugars!

Attic has a cozy room for Unikitty

White picket fence

EMMET'S DREAM HOUSE

Hopeful about the future, Emmet builds himself a cute house to live in with Lucy, Unikitty, and his houseplant, Planty. His colorful home's many rooms include a brooding room for Lucy and a toaster room for unlimited toast and waffles. Yum!

REBUILDING THE FUTURE

Emmet uses his construction worker and Master Builder skills to create the house of his dreams in the Apocalypseburg wasteland. The white fence and flowers are a cheerful sight. He hopes Lucy likes it!

RIDING HIGH

Emmet has salvaged wheels, bricks, and other pieces from Apocalypseburg's ruins to build an awesome three-wheel-high Thricycle. From this high up, he can see all across the city!

Driver's seat with space for Planty

Stabilizer for use when parked

DID YOU KNOW?

Lucy reuses the Thricycle's wheels to build an even speedier vehicle to escape the aliens.

Three wheels make for a speedy ride

WHEELY USEFUL

When Apocalypseburg is under attack, Emmet fires a Thricycle wheel rim at the brick-chomping alien invaders. Sadly, his three-wheeler gets blown apart by a heart missile.

EMMET THE TOUGH GUY?

While everyone else in Apocalypseburg has toughened up, Emmet hasn't changed at all. But seeing his friends taken into space makes Emmet realize that if he wants to save them, now is the time to get tough!

NOT SO SPECIAL

When mysterious Sweet Mayhem arrives in Apocalypseburg to take away its leaders, she thinks Emmet is weak, simple, and less than special. But he will prove her wrong!

TO THE RESCUE!

With no one willing to help him find his friends, brave Emmet heads off into space with just Planty, his houseplant, for company.

PLANTY

Planty is Emmet's friend. They travel everywhere together!

SMASHING ESCAPE

Emmet meets a space traveler named Rex who shows him how to toughen up. Emmet learns to get out of dangerous situations by channeling his sad feelings into a punch to the ground.

EMMET'S RESCUE ROCKET

Loyal Emmet is determined to save his friends! He rebuilds his house into an awesome rocket ship, and blasts off into space to rescue them.

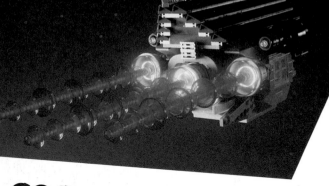

COSMICALLY COOL

Emmet adds three giant rocket engines, wings, weapons, and a control panel. Now he just needs to figure out how to fly the rocket ship!

Powerful rocket booster

Part of white picket fence from Emmet's house

Missile—for extra safety

LUCY

Lucy has always been tough, but she has had to become tougher than ever to survive life in Apocalypseburg. Forever a free spirit, Lucy is not a follower and questions everything.

THINGS YOU NEED TO KNOW ABOUT LUCY

1 She is a Master Builder—she can build anything out of anything.

2 Lucy is an expert at escaping capture. Her amazing backflips and jumping skills help!

3 She is a great team leader. She can always be relied on for coming up with a clever plan.

4 Lucy **really** dislikes the pop song "Everything is Awesome."

Rotating
arrow gun

Snazzy racing
stripes

DID YOU KNOW?

Lucy builds a very
angry Ultrakatty into
the car's motor to
give it even more
power.

THE GETAWAY CAR

Lucy and Emmet have to think quickly when they are under alien attack! They use the wheels from Emmet's destroyed Thricycle and bricks from the Apocalypseburg rubble to build a super-speedy escape buggy.

BUILDING TOGETHER

Lucy makes sure the car has a powerful turbo engine, while Emmet adds a safe tail light and blinker. They add large wheels and sturdy suspension to ensure a smooth ride—even over very bumpy terrain!

BATMAN

If anyone can look awesome during an alien invasion, it's this crime-fighting Super Hero! Proud Batman usually likes to work solo, but when Apocalypseburg is under attack, he teams up with everyone to save the city.

THINGS YOU NEED TO KNOW ABOUT BATMAN

1 The awesome Super Hero defends Apocalypseburg from his turreted fortress.

2 His fortress has a light-up sign that flashes "You're welcome" when he saves the day.

3 Flattery will get you everywhere with Batman.

4 He thinks the Queen of the Systar System is "rad."

31

BENNY

Spaaaaaceship! Building spaceships is Benny's favorite thing to do. The cheerful classic spaceman loves spaceships so much that he doesn't mind being taken by aliens ... because he gets to travel in an awesome spaceship!

THINGS YOU NEED TO KNOW ABOUT BENNY

1 The battle-worn Master Builder has had to build himself a new arm.

2 Benny is clumsy—keep away when he is wielding a blowtorch!

3 He has a crack in his helmet. No wonder he is often light-headed.

4 His battle cry against the DUPLO aliens is ... you guessed it ... "Spaaaaaceship!"

SPACESHIP WORKSHOP

Spaceship. Spaceship. SPACESHIP! Benny and Emmet build and fix up spaceships and other vehicles to use in the fight against the alien invaders. Benny's always ready to battle in space!

Space buggy

Tool cart

Emmet's buggy

DID YOU KNOW?

Benny wears his blue spacesuit, helmet, and oxygen tank at all times.

Fuel pump

Booster

SPACE SQUAD

The Queen of the Systar System promises Benny his own special world. There he can create the spaceship of his dreams with his very own spaceship-building team!

35

UNIKITTY

Super-cute Unikitty usually likes to think only of positive things, but she finds herself getting angrier and angrier with Apocalypseburg under attack. She uses these negative feelings to fight to defend the city with her friends.

THINGS YOU NEED TO KNOW ABOUT UNIKITTY

1 Unikitty is part-unicorn, part-kitten.

2 She is a Master Builder who loves to build cute, rainbow-colored, sparkly things.

3 Glitter, rainbows, butterflies, puppies, her friends, and spas make Unikitty happy.

4 People who put raisins in otherwise delicious food make her unhappy.

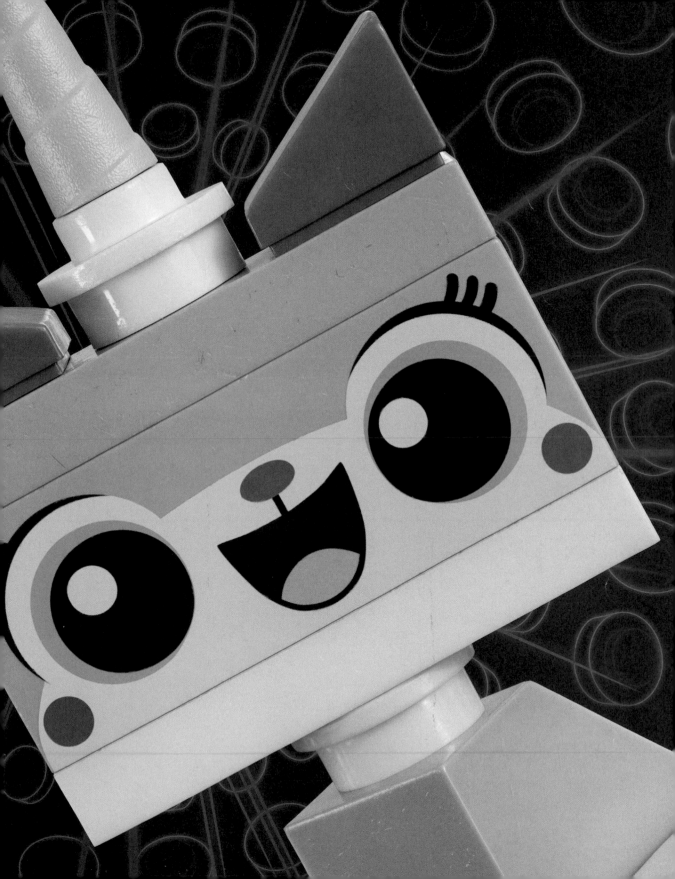

ULTRAKATTY

When Unikitty gets very angry, she channels her rage to transform into Ultrakatty—a big, bad fighting machine. Watch out, alien invaders! The fierce fighter just has to keep thinking angry thoughts, or she will turn back into sweet Unikitty.

ANGRY KITTY

When the aliens invade, Unikitty finds herself losing control of her positive thoughts and becoming Warrior Kitty. She uses this to her advantage by transforming into fearsome Ultrakatty.

WARRIOR DUO

Lucy hops onto Ultrakatty's back to ride into battle against the chomping DUPLO aliens. Ultrakatty shoots a flare from her horn to signal their friends for help.

SWEET SELF

Once the battle is over, Unikitty returns to her cute pink self ... until she gets angry again!

METALBEARD

With a body made up of a hodgepodge of pirate-ship parts, junk, and a collection of weapons, MetalBeard is well prepared when the aliens attack. He just hopes he doesn't lose any more body parts ...

THINGS YOU NEED TO KNOW ABOUT METALBEARD

1 The only parts of MetalBeard's original body that remain are his head and vital organs.

2 He stores his organs in his treasure chest.

3 MetalBeard is the captain of *The Sea Cow*, his very own pirate ship.

4 He loves having a spa scrub treatment—there is no better way to get your barnacles scrubbed off.

Crow's nest and flag

DID YOU KNOW?
Sweet Mayhem turns one of the shooting shark weapons into a harmless dolphin!

Shark shooter

Rotating turret with huge cannons

METALBEARD'S CHOPPER

Ahoy there! MetalBeard has built himself into an awesome battle vehicle. The chopper is built from pirate-ship parts and other random pieces— including a missile launcher that shoots snapping sharks at alien invaders!

BUILDING BLUNDER

Benny helps MetalBeard build the chopper. Unfortunately, he accidentally blowtorches MetalBeard's chest while working on it!

REX

Rex likes danger, traveling through space, and wearing vests. This tough, galaxy-hopping space pilot, archaeologist, cowboy, and raptor trainer does not like to talk about his past ... except he tells everybody at any opportunity!

THINGS YOU NEED TO KNOW ABOUT REX

1 Rex is a highly skilled pilot.

2 He helps Emmet to safety by flying him through a scary area of space known as the Stairgate.

3 Rex escapes danger by using his signature ground punch.

4 He always looks good in photographs.

LESSONS FROM REX

Emmet is awestruck by Rex when he meets him. He wants to learn to be tough just like him! Rex is flattered to teach Emmet, but it might be hard—sweet, innocent Emmet has a lot to learn!

1 Learn and practice a signature escape move for when you need to get out of dangerous situations.

2 Be decisive. Always act like you are right—even if you are not so sure!

3 Look ahead to the future.

4 Always wear a vest.

5 Learn a cool handshake.

6 Grow some stubble.

RESULT

Emmet gets tougher and gains the confidence to make decisions. But he ultimately realizes that being kind is a strength, too. Friends work better together with their different strengths.

EMMET

THE REXCELSIOR

Rex built this huge spaceship himself out of spare pieces he found. Just as tough-looking as its owner, the ship resembles a fist, and really packs a punch!

Worn-out paint

DID YOU KNOW?

As well as space cannons and a hyper-light-speed combuster, the ship has its own skate park!

Ship is made from hundreds of scavenged pieces

Enormous thruster

DINO CREW

The *Rexcelsior* has an unusual crew—a team of raptors that Rex has trained! Power up and crank the warp drive up to eleven, dinos!

16+

REX'S RAPTORS

Rex prefers to explore space alone, so he has trained a pack of raptors to be his faithful crew. They pilot his spaceships, carry heavy weapons, and scan new planets for danger.

THINGS YOU NEED TO KNOW ABOUT REX'S RAPTORS

1 Rex likes to name his raptors.

2 Attach high-tech wings to a raptor and it becomes a Rex-wing plane that flies in space.

3 These dinosaurs love to skateboard!

4 Rex's raptors are surprisingly affectionate, especially if you pet their bellies.

"It's not like anything we've ever seen ... What is it up to?"

—Lucy

SWEET MAYHEM

This mysterious space pilot is General Mayhem, Intergalactic Naval Commander of the Systar System. The sparkly armored warrior has arrived in Apocalypseburg on a secret mission. She may be named Sweet Mayhem, but this unwelcome visitor does not appear to be very sweet at all!

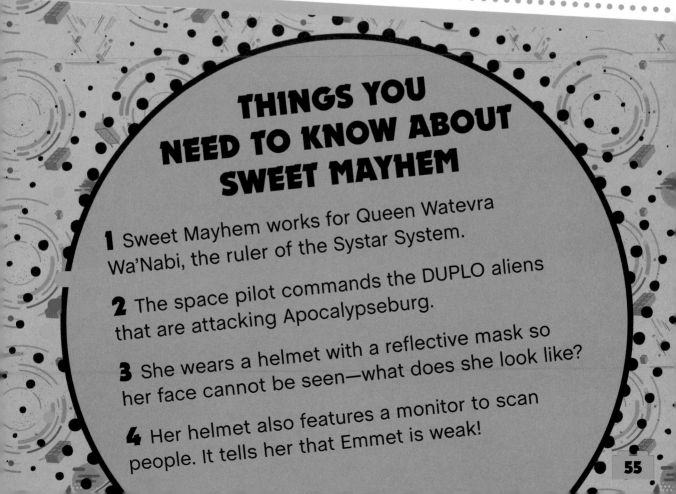

THINGS YOU NEED TO KNOW ABOUT SWEET MAYHEM

1 Sweet Mayhem works for Queen Watevra Wa'Nabi, the ruler of the Systar System.

2 The space pilot commands the DUPLO aliens that are attacking Apocalypseburg.

3 She wears a helmet with a reflective mask so her face cannot be seen—what does she look like?

4 Her helmet also features a monitor to scan people. It tells her that Emmet is weak!

SECRET MISSION

Sweet Mayhem has been sent to Apocalypseburg to gather its greatest leaders. They are cordially invited to a Ceremonial Ceremony at 5:15. By "invited," she means taken to the Systar System in her spaceship!

"Bring me your fiercest leader."
—Sweet Mayhem

SPACE FOR FIVE

Sweet Mayhem can only fit five prisoners in her spaceship. She needs to figure out who the city's fiercest leaders are.

A STICKY SITUATION

This mission is tougher than it first seemed. Sweet Mayhem uses her heart grenades and sticker gun to stop the gang from attacking.

INTO SPACE!

Sweet Mayhem does not tell the prisoners why they are being taken to a secret ceremony. She just scoops up Lucy, Benny, MetalBeard, Unikitty, and Batman into her spaceship!

"**Nooooooooooooo!**"
—Emmet

THE FORMIDABALL

Beware the Formidaball! Sweet Mayhem's fearsome spaceship has a cell for prisoners and a cannon that shoots exploding heart and star missiles. And just when you think the ship is destroyed, it reassembles again—all by itself!

HEARTS ATTACK

The Formidaball makes its presence known by playing loud pop music and shooting out exploding heart missiles.

UNFRIENDLY FIRE
Apocalypseburg gets rained on by these not-so-cute hearts and stars.

Aerodynamic fin for speedy space travel

Ultra-strong bulletproof armor

Extendable blaster cannon

HEARTS AND STARS

HELLO!

LOVE YOU!

I LOVE YOU MORE!

Don't be fooled by Sweet Mayhem's adorable-looking talking hearts and stars. They smile and say something cute, but then they explode! Keep away from these menacing missiles.

YOU ARE SO HANDSOME!

HOORAY!

IT'S GETTING SO COLD!

SAD STAR

Emmet feels sorry for a trapped star, who says it is cold and in pain, so he sets it free. He does not realize that it is helping trick him into letting Sweet Mayhem break into Batman's fortress!

WELCOME TO THE SYSTAR SYSTEM

Behold, the Systar System! It is made up of eleven planets that circle a blue, watery sun. Representatives from each of the planets gather on the blue sun to meet with the Queen of the Systar System.

DID YOU KNOW?

The universal language of the Systar System is song.

WHOA!

The gang think the Systar System looks amazing when they first see it from Sweet Mayhem's spaceship. Well, everyone does apart from Lucy.

STRANGE BEINGS

All kinds of beings live in the Systar System, including DUPLO aliens, Anthropomorphians, Cutopians, Friendopolites, and Vampiruses.

QUEEN WATEVRA WA'NABI

Presenting Her Majesty, Queen Watevra Wa'Nabi, Empress of the Systar System. It can be hard to spot this not-evil Queen because she changes her form all the time, but she is usually the one wearing a crown.

THINGS YOU NEED TO KNOW ABOUT THE QUEEN

1 Most importantly, she is not evil, nasty, or a villain.

2 Lucy is very suspicious of the Queen. She talks too much about not being evil!

3 The Queen prefers song and dance to simply talking.

4 She has ordered aliens from the DUPLO planet to collect bricks from Bricksburg for her new Space Temple.

TRANSFORMING QUEEN

Queen Watevra Wa'Nabi can transform into anything! She rearranges her bricks into any object or animal she wants. She can be a horse, a crown, a train, a dog, a mallet, a butterfly, a scary tentacled monster ... Anything is possible!

FIRST IMPRESSIONS

The gang mistakenly think that the Queen is a beautiful woman named Susan when they meet. They discover that the Queen is actually the horse that Susan is riding!

ICE CREAM CONE

Ice Cream Cone at your service! Queen Watevra Wa'Nabi's hardworking butler is always by her side. The sweet assistant is very polite and professional—unless he gets chocolate sauce spilled on him. Then he just needs to chill.

THINGS YOU NEED TO KNOW ABOUT ICE CREAM CONE

1 He introduces the Queen to guests and conducts important ceremonies.

2 Ice Cream Cone is always first to alert the Queen of any intruders to the Systar System.

3 He gets nervous if there is an ice cream parlor nearby.

4 Unikitty thinks he is so sweet, she could eat him!

QUEEN WATEVRA WA'NABI'S CASTLE

Queen Watevra Wa'Nabi reigns over the Systar System from her majestic castle on the sun. The sun is made up of oceans, and the inventive aliens that live here create clever machines that are powered by water to operate the castle's technology.

SPLASH LANDING

You can only visit the castle in a spaceship. Visitors travel down a circular waterfall that parts to reveal a beautiful castle.

THRONE ROOM

The Queen rules from a large central throne room with her assistant, Ice Cream Cone. She has important meetings here with aliens from other planets.

BALTHAZAR

This sparkly vampire runs the Harmonic Transmutation Center where Queen Watevra Wa'Nabi sends new visitors to the Systar System. Balthazar is in charge of getting visitors to change their attitudes.

THINGS YOU NEED TO KNOW ABOUT BALTHAZAR

1 There is no need to be scared of him—he is an attractive, non-threatening vampire.

2 He thinks Lucy is a "grumpledumpuss" because she won't change her attitude.

3 Balthazar is an expert in meditation—learning to free the mind of all thoughts.

4 He is a super-cool DJ in his spare time.

SPA DAY!

Namaste. Welcome to the Harmonic Transmutation Center and Changing Chambers. Are you ready to embark on your transformational journey? Follow these five simple steps:

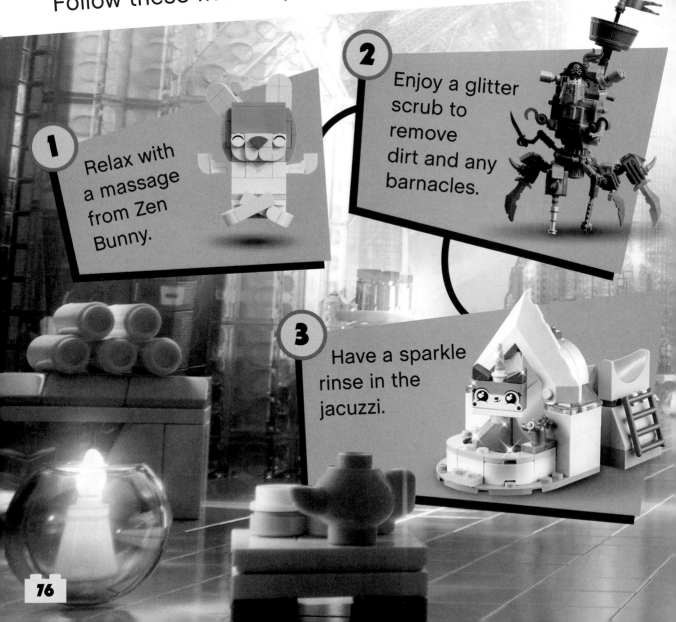

1 Relax with a massage from Zen Bunny.

2 Enjoy a glitter scrub to remove dirt and any barnacles.

3 Have a sparkle rinse in the jacuzzi.

4 Meditate with Balthazar. He will show you how to be in the moment.

5 Listen to a very catchy song—this is the very important final step in your transformation.

11

WHERE SHOULD YOU TRAVEL TO IN SPACE?

As Emmet knows, heading into space can be daunting. With so many planets to choose from, it is hard to know which to pick. Jump into your spaceship and use this handy quiz to help you make your decision.

Yes

Do you want to meet the Queen?

Yes

START
Are you looking for the Systar System?

No

No

Do you prefer nature to city life?

No

Yes

Apocalypseburg
This gloomy place is in ruins, but why not try to rebuild the city with your friends?

No

Space Temple
Go to the Space Temple to help the DUPLO aliens build for the Queen.

Queen Watevra Wa'Nabi's Castle
Head to the castle on the sun to meet Her Majesty, Queen Watevra Wa'Nabi.

Do you love castles?

Yes

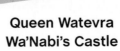

Yes

Harmony Town
You will fit in with life in this clean, peaceful, perfect town. Enjoy!

Are you super-sparkly clean?

No

Planet Sparkles
Visit this planet's incredible spa where you can relax, get clean, and be totally transformed!

The Jungle Planet
There is plenty of nature here. Beware the cute but menacing Plantimals though!

THE JUNGLE PLANET

Emmet and Rex arrive on a lush jungle planet to look for Emmet's friends. The pair become surrounded by adorable plantlike creatures. But these Plantimals are not at all cute, and they do not like intruders!

TROUBLE AHEAD

The raptors scan the area for danger and give Rex the all clear. They were mistaken! The Plantimals have sharp teeth and they are very hungry.

TRAPPED!

The creatures have long vines to trap intruders. Rex unleashes an almighty punch to the ground, which sends shockwaves through the jungle. The Plantimals retreat—phew!

"Only the toughest are going to get out of there alive."

—Rex

JUNGLE OFF-ROADER

Emmet thinks fast and uses the raptors' gear to build this cool off-roader to flee the attacking Plantimals. Luckily, Rex packed plenty of laser weapons. Pew pew pew pew!

All-terrain wheel

Rex's signature color scheme

NO FEAR

Rex often finds himself in dangerous situations, but he is always prepared. He wears his tough-guy gear, keeps his raptors close by, and loads the dinos with weapons and a danger-tracking device.

HARMONY TOWN

The perfect community of Harmony Town welcomes you! Discover rows and rows of colorful houses, beautifully mowed lawns, and the sparkliest, friendliest people you will ever meet.

PECULIAR PLACE

Emmet and Rex find themselves in Harmony Town when looking for the Ceremonial Ceremony and Emmet's friends. Harmony Town may look perfect, but there is something strange going on!

EPIC ESCAPE

Rex decides it is time to leave. The townspeople are acting weird. Emmet punches the perfect sidewalk and discovers outer space!

DID YOU KNOW?

Emmet sees a Harmony Town newspaper with the headline "Ceremonial Ceremony Today. Everything will change."

DOING IT HER OWN WAY

Lucy is strong, brave, and wary of strangers. She does not trust the leaders of the Systar System and refuses to follow their plans, unlike the rest of the gang. Lucy realizes that it will be up to her to defend her friends!

FEARLESS FIGHTER

Lucy is not afraid to charge at Sweet Mayhem and her barrage of flying stickers. She will do anything to protect her friends.

FOLLOW NO ONE

Benny, MetalBeard, Batman, and Unikitty may be excited to explore the Systar System, but Lucy is not!

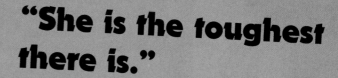

"She is the toughest there is."

—Emmet

BUILDING A PLAN

When Lucy worries that her friends are behaving strangely at the spa, she stays focused and alert. Quick-thinking Lucy will hatch a plan to rescue them.

LUCY'S GUIDE TO ESCAPING CAPTURE

Lucy must escape the spa to save her friends! Luckily, Lucy has had lots of practice in this area. The expert escapee just follows these steps.

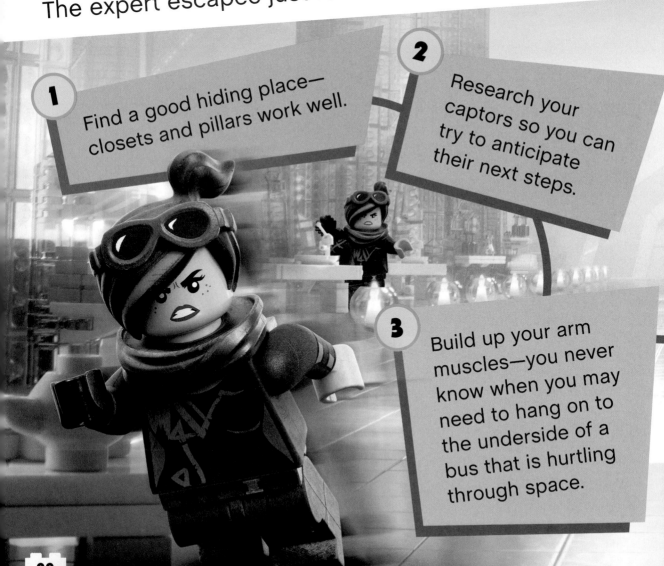

1 Find a good hiding place—closets and pillars work well.

2 Research your captors so you can try to anticipate their next steps.

3 Build up your arm muscles—you never know when you may need to hang on to the underside of a bus that is hurtling through space.

4 Practice backflips and jumps so you can move swiftly and quietly without being detected.

5 Dress the part—hoods and scarves work well when hiding.

6 Never feel fear.

"I'm having a great time!"
—Benny

Disco ball

Zebe, the driver, cranks up the volume

FUN BUS!

Benny, MetalBeard, Unikitty, and Batman are taken to the Ceremonial Ceremony on a bus. But this is no ordinary bus—it is a party bus that blasts very catchy music as it travels through space!

Rocket booster

POP-UP PARTY

There are more speakers than seats on the bus. The door and roof open to reveal a rotating dance floor. It's time to party!

TO THE RESCUE

Hooray! Emmet and Lucy find each other when they are both on the way to the Ceremonial Ceremony. Can they save their friends? And just what is Queen Watevra Wa'Nabi up to?

UNITING THE GALAXY

At the Ceremonial Ceremony, Lucy and Emmet learn that all is not as it seemed. The Queen and Sweet Mayhem have been trying to bring the galaxy together. Maybe they can all be friends and work together?

"We're not alone in this world."

—Emmet

WHICH SPACE ADVENTURER ARE YOU?

Some people are born to travel in space. Others need some encouragement! Take the quiz to find out what kind of space adventurer you would be.

1 What would your spaceship look like?

A. The best spaceship you have ever seen!

B. Homey and cozy with space for my friends.

C. Stylish with plenty of hidden weapons.

2 How would you describe your personality?

A. Space-obsessed

B. Cheerful

C. Mysterious

3 What is your favorite color?

A. Blue

B. Orange

C. Turquoise. Or pink. I can't decide!

4 Which kind of missions will you go on?

A. All kinds of space missions! I would travel into outer space every day if I could.

B. I would only ever go into space to rescue my friends.

C. Secret missions that I am not allowed to talk about.

MOSTLY As – BENNY

You LOVE space. There is nothing you do not know about space and building spaceships.

MOSTLY Bs – EMMET

You are friendly and loyal—and braver than you think! You can always be relied on to help your friends.

5 You get trapped by alien creatures on a dangerous planet. What do you do?

A. Hope my spaceship is very close by.

B. Build a vehicle to escape.

C. I would never get trapped. I would be trapping them!

MOSTLY Cs – SWEET MAYHEM

You are daring and adventurous. You can be trusted to take on top-secret space missions.

Senior Editor Helen Murray
Project Art Editor Jenny Edwards
Design Assistant James McKeag
Pre-Production Producer Marc Staples
Producer Louise Daly
Managing Editor Paula Regan
Managing Art Editor Jo Connor
Art Director Lisa Lanzarini
Publisher Julie Ferris
Publishing Director Simon Beecroft

Dorling Kindersley would like to thank Randi
Sørensen, Heidi K. Jensen, Paul Hansford,
and Martin Leighton Lindhardt at the LEGO
Group, and Ben Harper at Warner Bros.

First American Edition, 2019
Published in the United States by
DK Publishing
345 Hudson Street, New York, New York 10014

Page design copyright © 2019
Dorling Kindersley Limited
DK, a Division of Penguin Random House LLC

19 20 21 22 23 10 9 8 7 6 5 4 3 2 1
001–312558–Jan/2019

DORL41484
Manufactured by Dorling Kindersley
80 Strand, London, WC2R 0RL under license
from the LEGO Group.

Published in Great Britain by Dorling
Kindersley Limited

A catalog record for this book is available
from the Library of Congress.
ISBN: 978-1-4654-7966-2

DK books are available at special discounts
when purchased in bulk for sales
promotions, premiums, fund-raising,
or educational use. For details, contact:
DK Publishing Special Markets,
345 Hudson Street, New York, New York 10014
SpecialSales@dk.com

Printed and bound in U.S.A.

A WORLD OF IDEAS:
SEE ALL THERE IS TO KNOW

www.dk.com
www.LEGO.com